To Catch a Rainbow

– KATRINA SANDÈ –

An environmentally friendly book printed and bound in England by
www.printondemand-worldwide.com

This book is made entirely of chain-of-custody materials

www.fast-print.net/store.php

TO CATCH A RAINBOW

A catalogue record for this book is available from the British Library

ISBN 978-178456-058-4

First published 2014 by
FASTPRINT PUBLISHING
Peterborough, England.

Acknowledgments

Sincere thanks to my family, friends, Pam K and medical teams who helped me get through dark and difficult times. They showed me the way to a bright and healthier future. Without their help, I would not be here to tell my story.

Putting this book together has been a great challenge. They always showed keen interest in my writing and kept me going.

I hope that by reading this book, I will give other people who are in a similar situation, the strength to know they are not alone on the hard, gruelling battlefield against cancer.

My aim is to inspire them to keep strong, have faith, and most of all, not to lose the will to survive.

A very special thank you to my granddaughter Jean for encouraging me to put my journey fighting cancer onto paper. She is the one who ignited the spark for the flame of my life to burn on and on, like the Olympic torch, alight for the whole world to see.

"We are on this world once, Nan," she said. "Make your mark. Live life to the full."

Dedication

To my mother, a wonderful woman.

Listening to your beautiful soft voice, reading to us when we were young, inspired me to put words onto paper. You opened many doors for me.

Thank you, Mum.

Early Life

Katrina was born in Cornwall, southwest England in a small cottage close to the sea, where the air was fresh and the scenery beautiful.

The youngest of four children, Katrina was doted on by her older sister and two brothers. Her childhood was secure with responsible, loving parents who worked hard to make life comfortable for their family. Her father was in the wholesale business. Exporting and importing goods kept him busy, so time spent with his family was limited. This was where Katrina's mother took over. She had a love for reading, so when she could, she would take the children to the seafront to sit on the golden sands or the nearby park with packed lunches, a blanket and a good book to read to her young ones. Between them, the parents created a balanced, happy life. Katrina was lucky to have love, friends and beautiful surroundings to look back on.

As the years passed and the children became individuals, Katrina's love for the written word grew. She not only read, but also ventured out to write. Poetry was a hobby that opened new doors for her to explore and portray her feelings openly on the page.

After passing her O-levels, Katrina took further studies and qualified as a nursery nurse, working in schools with young children, which she loved.

It was there where she met a young man, Bryan,

who was to become her husband, friend and soulmate.

She is now happily married and has brought up her family of five children. Since then, she has been blessed with many grandchildren and great grandchildren, amongst her ups and downs with health.

It is wonderful for her to look back and be able to see the pleasures of love and achievement that she has been a part of. She feels humble and immensely grateful for these priceless gifts. Now she enjoys life and tries to make each day count.

"Love is free, free as a bird,
Love is like a song, that is good to be heard."

Words that mean so much to Katrina.

"To Catch a Rainbow" is a reflection of her life and how she handled living with, and surviving cancer. She feels honoured to be able to tell her story, hoping to give inspiration to those who may have lost the will to fight, or feel very isolated and need help. She would like to give back something to the world and the many people who helped her through her journey back to good health. Donating the proceeds from this book to the charities *Macmillan Trust* and *Cancer Research* is her way of thanking everyone involved in where she is at this present time.

Where we come from, nobody knows,
Where we go to, everyone goes.

We inherit this great earth as humans. It is our life and the way of living. Most certainly, we all look up to see the same sun and moon. In that sense, we are equal.

Humanity is what we practise and live by, but our separate thoughts, feelings, care and love is what makes us individuals; each unique person having a role to play in this great universe.

We will make our journey through life and travel on a road which will lead us to the same destination.

The difference is how we take this journey and which path we choose. Sometimes paths are already set for us and it is not possible to reverse them. Such is the work of our creator.

Some believe in fate or destiny. Whichever way we look at it, this is what life is all about.

As the saying goes, "The spice of life, could be nice, could be full of pain and strife."

Spices of life have many different colours, textures and tastes, hot and cool, to relish and savour, but some are sour to the tongue; spices we do not want to taste or even touch as they will burn our skin. Life is just so full of goodness and badness, happiness and sadness.

Many people will travel life's road to reach their goal without any hiccups, but there are also some unfortunate ones who will have many obstacles to overcome on their way. They will taste both the bitter and sweet spices which life throws at them, hopefully having the strength and courage to pick up and carry on.

I have had the misfortune of being in the firing line with illness. Of living and fighting cancer twice in my life, but luckily surviving it.

I count myself truly blessed. I am humble, and thankful to be able to tell and portray the journey I made to a better future than that which I was expecting.

I hope that reading this book will be of help to the many people who have been affected by cancer.

Cancer is one of the major causes of worry, distress, trauma and hopelessness. Many people are affected, but do not know how to cope with all the anxiety and pressure it brings.

We may not be able to cure all the cancers that exist, but we can, by opening our hearts, sharing, caring and supporting others with knowledge and experiences, help others to deal with it more positively, to live and fight it.

So this book will tell my side of the story, of how I took it knowing I had cancer, how I dealt with it, my frailties, my anger and feelings of negativity. This was alongside the loving support and endless belief of my family and friends, who encouraged me to stay focused and strong enough to pull myself through the dark and difficult periods of my life when I felt fragile and lost. They will always be the reason I wake up each day.

I reflect on the time when I found out that I had cancer. I felt so low and negative about almost everything.

I didn't know if the next day would come for me, if I would see another beautiful sunrise, or bask on the beach with the person I love, to behold a golden setting of an evening sun and experience together the ending of another day; special moments I held close to my heart.

Were they gone forever? Would these magic moments never be relived? So many thoughts came to my mind at that time.

I mused over our holidays to other countries and the trips we made regularly. We visited churches to pay our respects to all religions, as we shared the belief as one that everybody is equal, and has the same right to opinions in the world, so long as they respect each other and live side by side harmoniously.

All of this was preying on my mind. There was disruption and mayhem in my life. Happiness was suddenly being whisked away from me.

Where was my God for me?

Part I - So My Story Starts: 1985

Looking back to the time when I first had cancer.

I was young then, and quite naïve to all the problems that one could have in life. All I knew were the basic facts of being healthy, with only occasional setbacks such as colds, flu and other minor illnesses.

There was nothing extremely bad or life-changing that I could envisage. It was a good time!

I was married at seventeen, my husband eighteen. We had our son a year later.

I recall May 25th, our son's twenty-first birthday.

My life then consisted of the happiness of being parents and new grandparents-to-be. We were very lucky to have these pleasures to look forward to. It was our son's child on the way, the first grandchild in our family, a very exciting time for all of us. It was a small gathering of just our immediate family, with lots of cakes and snacks. We were planning to hold a massive party once the baby was born; not long to wait. We still celebrated our happy occasion with love and laughter, and made our special day memorable.

Little did I know how times would change for us.

It was just one week later, in the early hours of the morning, when our nephew came banging on our front door, screaming and shouting. All we could gather was that his father, my husband's brother, wouldn't wake up. My husband flew out of the house to his car and drove as fast as he could with his nephew to his brother's house which was a few minutes away. During those horrific moments, there was panic and mayhem.

My son ran barefoot to his uncle's house, as he knew that no-one would have knocked on our door at that time of the morning unless something was very wrong.

The most shocking, unexpected thing had happened. My husband's brother had passed away. We were devastated and inconsolable. He was only forty-two and fit and healthy.

The next few weeks were so sad and painful only God knew how we coped. As a closely knit family, we went through the rituals of losing the eldest and most respected brother, son and father. A great man, looked up to by all around him. It was a hard loss to take.

Picking up the courage to carry on and keep the family together was difficult at that time. Our spirits were low. Another day would begin and lonely nights return. Every day would bring more painful duties to fulfil, to comfort members of the family, each with their individual losses, including our own. They were dark, stark days. The light of my husband's life, his older brother had gone, never to return.

It was one of the hardest times we lived through.

But that was not all. More grief was yet to come. Just two weeks later, June 17th, our dear grandmother, who had suffered with a stroke and was hospitalised, also passed away. We did regret that we were not by her side as much as we would have liked, but due to my brother-in-law's death, we were not physically able to go and stay with our gran. It was sad and her presence would be sorely missed, bless her. The only consolation to us was that she had limited use of her faculties with disabling ailments, and indeed was suffering. Poor gran was kept from knowing about the sad death of her eldest grandson. She would not have been able to take that shock.

Two deaths so close to each other; another painful period of lamenting. Sometimes, we would just sit around in silence, reflecting on our life before all of this tragedy. We mostly stayed together round my brother-in-law's house. There, we consoled each other, feeling closer to him.

At home, our own children coped on their own. For them, there was nothing much to do, but bide their time until the baby arrived. We lost the spark of excitement and expectancy of a newborn precious baby that would be arriving in our house soon. How the cards had changed for us!

I now realise that, because of this traumatic disruption to our life, I had not been taking the symptoms I was experiencing with my health seriously enough. A while before all of this, I had been to the doctors and had tests done, but never thought much about them. In my mind, I would be given medication and the problem would go. So I thought!

The days passed like months for us. People still came to pay their respects. This would bring a change to the day, as by talking, we were letting out our anguish and grief, enough to pull us through the next day.

July 3rd was our wedding anniversary, but we were not up to doing anything special, so it just went by.

A few days earlier, I had received an appointment from the hospital to see a consultant on July 4th. I was going to try and miss this. I was feeling low. What good would this do me? However, my husband and the family knew about the appointment and I was forced to attend. Maybe they thought it could be serious. Attending would put our minds at rest.

So I gathered my thoughts about myself. I did notice that I had been feeling worse as the days went on. Emotionally hurt as well as physically in pain and discomfort.

It was unusual for my husband to accompany me to the hospital, but the women of the house were not up to going with me.

The time came to see the consultant. The nurse who called my name out actually asked if there was anyone with me. I nodded and beckoned my husband to accompany me. "Very unusual," I thought.

As we were led to the seats in front of the consultant, I noticed the seriousness written on his face. My heart dropped.

"Well, my dear," he said, "you do have cancer, and it is quite aggressive. The treatment is fast and tough."

He paused, giving us time to let it sink in. I immediately looked across to see my husband's face. He had turned very pale. I grabbed hold of his hand and squeezed it tightly.

"Look Bryan," I said, shaking inside, but outside remaining as firm as I could, "I don't feel ill, I'll be okay."

He looked back at me so hurt and shocked with a look I'll never forget. Seconds of silence seeming like ages. Our eyes met and with mutual inner thoughts, our souls became one. Such is love.

His world had turned over, but he uttered, "We'll fight this together."

I knew my husband was fragile and vulnerable at that time. He had taken so many knocks lately, and this was the closest and most affecting, to know that, I, his wife and life partner, was ill with cancer. I was his pillar to lean on and we had pulled through the darkest times as one.

We faced the consultant again. He had waited patiently for us to accept the news.

I was to be sent for cesium treatment, another form of radiation, after which I would have radiotherapy administered in another hospital located forty miles away, as there was no closer medical facility for this type of treatment. A journey of eighty miles a day for five weeks!

We walked out of the hospital with heavy, troubled hearts. During the journey home, I noticed my husband's driving was not right. He almost knocked over bollards which were on our side of the road. Still, he carried on, but adjusted himself to driving safely again.

I was feeling sick, but managed to control myself. "I've got to be strong," I whispered quietly to myself. "For you, my love, for me and for my dear family."

We drove straight to his brother's house where most of the elders were, including his mother who was waiting expectantly to hear the outcome of our visit to the hospital. They were just as shocked and devastated to learn that more worry was to besiege the family, for all of us to bear.

The rest of the day was hard, tiring, emotional and difficult to get accustomed to. Deep inside, my own emotions were playing havoc with me.

I was screaming silently, "Did I have to have cancer? Why should I have cancer? Why me?" Especially at the time when I needed to be there for the coming of our precious grandchild.

Tears that should have been shed were held back, and could not be expressed to relieve my pain. Then, as God would have it, I realised that our own children looked to us for guidance and strength. How could we let them down? So out came the mother in me and I hugged each one of our children, with words of comfort, telling them not to worry, everything would be alright. They were old enough to understand the situation we were facing and responded with encouraging words from their hearts.

It was the first time we had stayed at our own home for a long while, but even as we went to bed, sleep was not to come. We lay awake reflecting on the day's events that had changed our lives in such a short time.

My heartbeats were so irregular. One minute my heart would pound so fast, and the next it would seem as if it had stopped. At least I could tightly hold on to my husband and feel his presence. It made me feel a little stronger.

How was I to know what other wounds I would suffer, or wars I would have to fight?

The next day brought tragic news that my own mother had passed away in the early hours of the morning; such a shock that I became speechless and numb. How could this be? Was I dreaming?

The cries coming from inside were as if they belonged to someone else, only it was me.

People, voices all around me, were saying, "Be strong, hold on, you have to go through so much yet."

I could not comprehend all this pain, and I collapsed, broken and shattered.

Later, when the situation was in hand, we received the news in bits and pieces. The fact was, mother had suffered a massive stroke - so tragic. She was only sixty-six years of age, a beautiful elegant woman, whom I admired. She inspired me to keep myself fit and trim as she did, even after having such a big family. She was my guardian angel who would have pulled me through thick and thin, especially at this time when I needed her.

"Oh, Mum, where are you now?" my heart cried.

How could it be? Was I never to see my mother again? My mind was in turmoil. How would I carry on? God help me!

As if God heard me, I looked again at my own offspring. They were helplessly overcome with the news and the way I took it. I bore an inner strength again, telling me how to hold onto myself for the sake of my children. My cries died down as I saw my daughter-in-law, bless her. She looked so worried and worn out. My maternal instinct took over. I calmed down, exhausted, silently crying. That evening went by solemnly, quietly reflecting on the day's events. It was time we all needed.

More hurdles were to come. We had to go to Bristol to see my side of the family. It was one of the most difficult times I can remember.

The family understandably was distraught. As for me, I was not only mourning the passing away of my heroine, my dear mother, but inside my heart was aching to be released from the knowledge that I would have to attend hospital in the next couple of days to undergo treatment for cancer. These silent thoughts were the cause of my distress. I would have openly confided my worries to my sisters, but to see them so upset over Mother made me withhold my news. Only further heartache would have come out of it.

My husband and younger brother-in-law, a doctor, took charge of the situation and explained to the family the importance of me returning home. Bless them, they did as they were asked, and sadly we set off. I only had a short time to express my grief and condolences to my immediate family, as I was not well enough to take any more on. It was as if I was living in a nightmare land. I was being led here, there and everywhere physically by my husband and his faithful brother.

The journey home was so long, it seemed never ending. Still in a state of shock and denial, I felt cold and numb. All I could do to keep warm was wrap myself up in a thick blanket.

What an unbelievable situation! Three deaths in the family in just five weeks. On top of all that, knowing I had cancer and an uncertain future. Could it be cured? Would I survive it or was that the end of me?

Over the next few days, I had to prepare myself physically and mentally for the ordeal facing me, the treatment to try and stop the cancer spreading and to kill what was there, hopefully. But would I survive? What would become of my family if I didn't pull through? Would I get to see our precious grandchild? While I lay on my bed tired and feeling hopeless, these questions rolled over in my mind umpteen times.

Looking back, I think losing my mother was when I completely went to pieces. That was when whatever strength I had was knocked out of me. I think if she had been alive, I would have had her shoulder to lean on. I know my family were there for me, but to have my own mother's comforting words, company and support would have made the load easier to bear. It was as if I had a massive gap in my soul. Would it ever be filled again? I was hurting so much, I started to repeat to myself, "Dear God, Dear God." I needed my maker to help pull me through. I had to search somewhere for faith and that was when I turned to the creator, the one who put us on this great world. Only he knows where our destiny lies.

I reflect now how selfish it was of me. I knew I felt the loss of Mum so much, but she did have a big family who would greatly miss her presence and kind loving nature. And then there was my father who loved Mum with a passion hard to believe. He still doted over her, and they had spent most of their time in each other's company, just under fifty years of marriage. How he would miss her! These were consoling feelings to get me through the early days of bereavement.

July 12th, the day for admission to hospital arrived. My husband came with me. Arriving in the ward, we held hands as often as we could. He was always there for me, and knowing that made me feel a little stronger. I had left home with the family's good wishes, gentle hugs and kisses and words of comfort, such loving support! I vowed I would try to be strong for them. We as a family had so much to look forward to. The baby was due in a week's time. Hopefully I would be home to witness this precious occasion. I tried lifting my spirits.

On the admission day, many different procedures were done; injections, blood samples, doctors coming to take down notes as to when I started noticing symptoms, how many children I had, how long I had been married, at what age I was married. So many questions were asked.

It was when my husband had left for the day that I felt alone and fragile. It came to the crux when another doctor came to talk about the procedure the next day. Then the pressure became unbearable. I could take no more. I broke down and cried my eyes out. I remember how loud and forceful it was. I could not control it. The doctor let me cry. He made no attempt to stop me.

When I could cry no more, he held my hand and asked how I was feeling and if there was anything else worrying me. I slowly told him my experience of the last five weeks, and to top all of that, my mother's passing away only a week ago. He was very concerned and noted it all down for their own records. Later, he gave me a sedative to help me relax.

The next day, the cesium treatment began. It was a form of radiation, and had to be retained outside my body for one hundred and one hours precisely. I was not allowed out of bed for that period of time. My diet was special, and I had tubes to see that my body fluids were working as they should.

From that day, I was given the utmost attention by doctors, nurses and the small amount of relatives, my husband, my mother-in-law and brother-in-law, who were the only ones allowed to visit me. It was because of the danger of being exposed to radiation that I was kept isolated.

It was 1985 and Live Aid was being televised. Bless the staff, to make me feel a little less lonely they arranged for a small television to be placed in the room, hung high on the wall so nothing was in the way of the tubes attached to me. The sides of the bed were also raised so I could not accidentally fall out.

The time passed slowly but surely. With the help of my God and the loving care and attention of everyone, I pulled through the week of gruesome treatment.

The day before being allowed home, I was given another anaesthetic to remove the tubes. I was very grateful and felt humble to be taken such good care of.

Before returning home, my wish was to give the hospital, a token of gratitude; a special thank you to the doctors who use their knowledge and skill to regularly save patients, wholeheartedly and with compassion. Also to the hard working, kind and helpful staff, trying to cheer people up with their care and smiles. I told my husband my wishes. He then bought what I asked. Along with a thank you card, my husband had purchased a huge bouquet of fresh flowers and two big tins of Roses chocolates.

My homecoming was a welcome I would remember for a long time to come. My children made nice food and brightened up the living room so it would be pleasing to my eyes. The biggest surprise was that our bedroom was completely refurnished and the bed was replaced by a beautiful bigger one. I was amazed that so much had been going on to please me, making me forget what I had being going through during the last week. I thanked them. Everyone had played a part with their love for me.

My whole being will never forget the support I was given. Reflecting back, I still thank all those who were there for me. I was not alone in my darkest hours. Even though I did not feel it, there was someone holding me. Now I know, it was my maker, he who writes our Kismet. I was destined to see much more in life.

In the days that went by, I adjusted to a different lifestyle. Tired and still low, I pottered around the house, keeping my mind busy. Inside, my heart felt a longing to be normal again. To have happy times. Where were they all gone?

Bless the family. Again, they all came to see me to keep my spirits up. Even my sister-in-law left her house to come to me. It was as if she needed me as much as I needed her, we were both going through a traumatic and tragic time. We shared our heartaches and opened up to share our mutual feeling. Indeed, she was my friend and companion.

I was not to know that when my son heard about me having cancer, he could not face me nor speak to me of his hurt, shock, and distress at the outcome of my illness. So when he did come, he left so suddenly, I was left wondering what, if anything, I may have said to him to make him shy away and leave so abruptly like that.

Later, I learned that it was his way of blocking out reality. He was unable to face the fact that his mother was so poorly, and that he could not physically do anything to make things right.

He was always a mender, a man of strength and might, but in this situation, he felt helpless. News of my cancer had left him shattered. His world had been turned upside down during the past few weeks, coping with three deaths in the family, and the responsibility he had to take on, keeping his brothers and sisters together, holding the fort. This was the limit. At twenty one, he and his beautiful wife were expecting their first child. This should have been a precious time for us as a closely knit family to enjoy. Where would I be in the next few weeks? Would I get better? What would become of them if things took a turn for the worse? What would be the consequences if I did not make it? His wife needed me at a crucial part of her life.

These unanswered questions tormented him.

Anger and fear set in his young mind.

That was when this happened.

***

Fear Can Close Many An Open Door

You looked at me with searching eyes,
As if something was on your mind,
Then, as if a small spark,
Something clicked,
The words you could not find.
    That moment I remember well,
    I saw the child in you that day,
    You looked so young and fragile,
    As suddenly you rushed away.
What was it you were running from
That made you go like that, my son?
It felt as if we were not that close,
Or lived and loved as mother and son.
    I know that time is of the essence,
    I know it was for you that day.
    If I could have made that time stand still,
    Just to hear what you had to say.
My heart says there is something wrong,
But how can I make it right?
If I knew what the problem was
I would help you fight the fight.
    So please come back and tell me so,
    Don't let time pass away,
Open your heart, I'm here for you,

Say the words you want to say.
Come what may, my son,
We hope to live and see a better day.
Enough to see good times again,
The sun will shine after pouring rain.
Most of all as always
Our love as mother and son will remain.

Thankfully, as time passed on, he was kind and considerate towards me, but refused to talk openly about my illness. It was as if there was an opaque curtain between us, marring us from seeing each other in a clear light, a gap between our mutual feelings.

Every now and then, as if a gentle breeze would blow, the curtain would be lifted and closeness returned. Simply by a hug, or the grasping of my hand before leaving, I had the knowledge that we were on the same wave length again. I suppose, because the cancer was in a personal and private part of me, it was difficult to talk openly about it. However, even during this silent behaviour, I could still feel the love and warmth of my precious son again.

The day came, July 23rd, when our grandchild was born. I will never forget the happiness God had bestowed on us as a family. Our son and daughter-in-law were blessed with a beautiful baby boy and us, a precious grandson. How humble and honoured we were to receive a gift such as this. He would be our future and carry our name on. He brought such joy and relief to us.

Now we were able to see changes in our sad, uprooted life.

We had something to hold and cherish. A new baby was in our house. I must say, he brought smiles to our faces. My heartfelt gratitude was to our son and daughter-in-law, pulling together at our time of need and keeping the family in a positive frame of mind. I think they matured quickly, and had to be strong to get to this stage of life. They truly deserved this happiness. I vowed from then on, God willing, I would be there for them and enjoy our times as one big family as much as we could.

Max, our grandson, was the light of our life. Each day made a difference for the better. Slowly, we came back to life again. He was the reason we woke up each day. We had many hours of fun and managed to smile once more.

Still at times, I had moments of feeling low. I would feel the losses we had suffered. Moments of sadness would rise, and I felt the need to express my sorrow. I would sing beautiful lullabies to our grandson, but in a low voice. Though it was extreme happiness that I experienced, holding him in my arms, inside I was still sad, but also healing. The torn scars were slowing mending with the pure love I had for our little grandson and our family. He was our saviour, a lifeline God had sent.

We prayed to be strong, hold on, move forward, for our future generation relied on us as elders and examples.

With this intention, we began to gain faith again. Holding on and saying that there was light at the end of the tunnel.

The next five weeks were very full. It was moments of joy in the company of little Max, then a long journey to hospital for radiotherapy treatment. By the end of the day, I would be tired and looking forward to a rest in bed, having to face another day with the same routine. This carried on every week day, leaving the weekends to recuperate and prepare for the oncoming week's treatment, very regular, to make the healing as effective as possible. At the hospital, I would meet patients with the same illness. While waiting for our turn, we would talk about our separate cancers which had to be treated with radiotherapy. Amazing how many people were in the same situation! I made friends who kept in touch with me for a long time after.

Day by long day, it was getting more tiring for me. By the end of the last session of radiotherapy, I was exhausted. Thank God that stopped! Next, I was given appointments to see my consultant for constant checkups. At least I would have breathing space between visits to the hospital. From now on, time would be a healer.

Life most certainly carries on. It is how we take the day and what we make of it that counts.

Max was our lifeline. We hung on to the happiness we had and relished in good days ahead. Slowly, I recuperated enough to take the family out to the parks again and enjoy special times. The happiness we thought would never come was in our hands again at last.

Life, as we all know is never perfect, but to take the good times with the bad makes living easier.

With our minds focused on looking forward and not back, we managed to put the fractured pieces of our lives together by mending them with love and the remaining strength we retained from surviving the tempestuous storms that had hit us not so long ago. Day by day, we would find other projects to pursue, such as decorating our front room, mowing the lawn, sowing new seeds and planting flowers. All good things to bring the freshness of a better and brighter future. The days would seem as normal as before. My strength was slowly returning. Although not as active as before, I could do many pleasurable things in life again.

The following years progressed steadily. Our grandson was now two years of age, a lively, happy young lad. The latter part of that year, our eldest daughter got married, and very soon we were expectant grandparents again, this time twice over, for our son and daughter-in-law were also expecting another child. These were good times.

My health was always kept in check. I was having hormone replacement tablets to balance the level of my hormones. These tablets had side effects; hot flushes, which I adjusted to by mostly wearing a shawl or removing it if I felt like it, and night sweats which were very uncomfortable, not only for myself, but for my husband who still insisted we stay living as a married couple.

Our bedroom was a refuge. Staying physically close to each other was a comfort which was lacking. I will always be grateful to him, as he was there for me day and night. Such is the power of love. As we had promised in our vows, "In sickness and in health." I truly was treated with love and compassion. He was, and still is my soulmate.

The medication I was taking, though essential, put me through early menopause. I was on these tablets for six years. I know that my body had taken its toll. Cancer made me grow older before my time, but it was better to have good health than to suffer and lose out on life altogether. I had learned this the hard way.

Just as sure as night turns into day and day into night, each day will come. It matters how we spend it.

I slowly grew stronger and regained the will to make something positive out of my life, to make natural progress to fulfil my desire to accomplish something to look back and say, "I did that." I was from a learned family, and grew up appreciating the written word, be it in poetry or prose. My love for writing is still with me.

The other aim was to pick up on the qualifications

I had from school and put them to further use in a career in the Education Department. My love for and with children in teaching and learning would be so good for me. It would give me back some confidence, to feel useful, a part of society. It was a step in the right direction, so I dedicated my time to studying for the N.N.E.B., a nursery nurse qualification, in my spare time whilst also working in a nursery school. This was the most positive step in a long time. I was beginning to enjoy living.

Our family could now get on with their own lives, leaving me and my husband to get on with ours. He carried on with his job as a financial planning consultant and I as a bilingual teaching assistant. Life again had meaning. We would all work in the day and get together as a big family at night. We were happy, but for how long?

It was April, 1991. Myself, my mother-in-law and daughter had the chance to go to India for a short break, and were fortunate enough to have booked our tickets to return just in time before our youngest son's first child arrived. My husband did not go with us on this occasion, so he held the fort at home.

However, things changed. Our daughter-in-law slipped and started labour two weeks before her time. It was not what we had planned. We were supposed to be home for the special occasion of our grandchild's birth, but fate is not controlled by our hands, but our maker's. We are only pawns in a game of chess. We have to stay where we are put.

Our son and daughter-in-law went through the early stages of parenthood without me by their side. This is another regret I will always have. They were blessed with a son, a truly precious gift of God.

At hospital, unusual things were happening. Our new grandson was having minor complications, but when we arrived home, he had settled. He was allowed home as routine. We made his homecoming as special as he was. The house was merry and we celebrated joyfully.

The next few days, I was going through jet lag, so time was all mixed up for me. Unknown to me, our little grandson was having breathing difficulties, but as the midwife had been to check on both mother and child earlier, there was nothing to worry about. However, a mother has her own instincts. By the afternoon, my daughter-in-law felt she had to wake me to say that the baby was not feeding and she was worried. I got myself up and went to see our little grandson. To me, he was looking poorly, enough to make me check him over thoroughly. First thing I noticed was that his lips were turning blue, and he was struggling to breathe, I was positive there was something very wrong.

"Get him to the hospital as fast as we can," my heart cried. Firmly, I said to my son, who was fortunately home at the time, "Take us to the hospital, he needs to be checked."

I held our grandchild, and at that moment, he was quiet and breathing very slowly. I prayed silently all the way to the hospital, stopping to say positive things to my children. They couldn't know how worried I was. We had to keep as calm as we could.

The journey was long, but we finally arrived. As we came into the hospital, we went straight to the desk. The admission receptionist stopped my son and daughter-in-law to ask routine questions. I was holding my grandson, and I knew there was something wrong. He needed to be seen as soon as possible.

I pushed past everyone in my way and screamed, "Someone look at our baby!"

Suddenly, the attention was on our grandson, and the doctors and nurses were all around him.

From that moment, there was so much going on. An oxygen mask was put on our precious grandson. Immediately, the appropriate doctors were called. We were led to another part of the hospital equipped for our baby's needs.

By this time, my husband had joined us. It was as if we were in a horrible nightmare. We were afraid of what was happening to our precious new baby. Every minute made a difference.

Scans were taken and studied at the same time. We were told there was a possibility that the baby's heart was not formed properly. This was a massive hit to take. No! No! It could not happen like this. Why? Why? So many questions firing in our minds. This sheer grief was agonising. We held each other for support. All four of us in a terrible dilemma.

My legs were shaking so much, I was about to fall, but when I looked at our children, I realised the shocking news was even harder to take for them.

"Don't let us let them down. Be strong for them. Hold on," I whispered to myself. "Dear God, dear God, please help us." God is great. He will mend broken pieces and make it whole. It is in His power, if He so wishes.

It was then when a young doctor, whom we believed was a messenger from God, came to us and said, "There is a way to solve this. We must act now and get him to Groby Road Hospital, Leicester, where the operation can be performed. It specialises in heart surgery."

A miracle had happened! We had something to hold on to! A hope, a prayer. In my mind I thought, "Thank you dear whoever you are up there for giving us that important link which might be the strongest to mend the chain of life and save our precious new baby."

It was immediately arranged that we travel through the night to Leicester in an ambulance. Time was of the essence, very crucial. Every second counted.

We were taken straight to the ward where our baby would have the life-saving operation. We learned that he had a coarctation (narrowing) of the aorta, the main artery leading from the heart. Our grandson had a bypass operation; so much to go through at such a young age. He truly was a soldier put through his paces in the early days of life.

Would he have the strength needed to make him better? We prayed with mind and soul to pull him through this troubled, disruptive world of entanglement; a dense jungle, where there was little light showing for him.

"Please make him better, let him out, give him a chance to see the beautiful sunshine that is out there in Your world. Give him a full life." These were my inner prayers to my creator who pulled me through when I needed Him. Surely He would hear me now.

I had a glimmer of faith. Yes, that is what makes us strong, to believe in what we want. That is the beginning of hope.

We all must have been silently hoping and praying, but our energy levels were low. Exhausted, there was nothing else we could do but sit and wait in the small room we were given.

Our own hearts ached to see our children, young as they were, so serious, tearful, looking lost and helpless, experiencing their first major hurdle in the early part of a wonderful marriage. It was only a year since their wedding. So many dreams to fulfil yet. Their baby, so new and precious, fighting for his life.

But our grandson was a fighter, even at that young age. With the feeling of being trapped and restricted, he used his strength and willpower that he was fortunate to be born with to heave him out of a horrible sinking well. He tried to pull off those lifesaving wires which obstructed him from moving freely. Even then, his spirit was strong enough to bear the pain and discomfort in his young life, and overcome major surgery to which he had been subjected. Slowly, through anxious weeks of patience and treatment, he made enough progress to the doctors' and surgeons' satisfaction.

We as a big family felt grateful, humble and gifted to receive him back home well again. Our whole house, close friends and community welcomed him with good wishes, blessings and presents. It was truly a miracle we had lived through.

To this day, he still has that air of magic around him. He has a special gift of writing, 'rapping' about so many subjects, way above his level, in lyrics that can only be described as wondrous, amazing and unbelievable for his age. People say he is a genius. We know him as an extraordinary young man with high values and qualities hard to find nowadays. He portrays wisdom and good manners, and lives by respecting others. His nature is kind, helpful and he has a personality which is outstanding. God had saved such a unique person at a very young age, as he was to be our role model and an inspiration to others.

When I look back, I am thankful to my creator for blessing me with such happiness I thought I would never achieve again. He is another reason to wake up each day.

It only shows,
We know not what tomorrow brings,
Good news, bad news, all sorts of things.
Yesterday has been, never to return,
We can only remember, and from that we can learn.
So why not
Change what we can,
Make better from the worst,
Then we would not have lived in vain
Our life would have purpose.
That period of time I will never forget.

***

That day was so special as we were celebrating my grandson's sixteenth birthday. He had gone through so much in his young life, having a heart bypass operation when he was just five days old. It is truly a miracle that he survived that ordeal, and is in good health now.

He is an amazing, unique person with so much knowledge and wisdom; qualities of strength and power which pulled him through that crucial time.

Knowing that, and thinking of the traumatic time in our lives, seeing our little grandson in this plight, the emotional journeys we took together as a family, overcoming the many obstacles in our way, made my own troubles seem small and insignificant. I put on a brave face for this celebration and truly felt blessed that I could see this occasion.

One day in my life I was happy as a bird,
My song of love could clearly be heard,
To all that were around me. And I felt good and
    free
From toil and trouble, reality.
My thoughts of sadness, that day
Brushed clear away,
Forgotten, I could honestly say,
Enjoying precious time with my family,
I was in ecstasy!
Sometimes, the emotions of love will conquer,
Over-ride negativity.

***

As the years flew by, the future seemed bright for me. Our children were young adults now. There were engagements, weddings and more grandchildren in our family. Happiness and a settled life had come to us once more.

We started to relax with a new outlook on life. It was then when we gathered the confidence to travel with the knowledge that our family could get on with life on their own.

So we booked short holidays abroad which were

thoroughly enjoyable. We travelled to so many parts of the world; Italy, Spain, Venice, and finally making more journeys to Portugal, a country we loved with beautiful scenery and very welcoming people.

It was there where my husband thought of our lifetime aspirations that one day we would build our own house, somewhere warm and sunny. It was a pie in the sky dream then, but having gone through so much with health issues, we decided to take action while we could, trying to make our dreams come true.

The project of buying land with a sea view came into being. When we finally agreed on the location and price, there were big steps to have the plans of a villa passed. And so our project began.

So much went on in the next few years. We made our holidays to Portugal as many times as we could to see our villa being built. Finally, our dream home was finished. We enjoyed our time there, inviting our families over to spend time with us. Those were good days, paradise! We were living our dream!

Life went on. By now we were growing older and keeping the villa was becoming more difficult because of the closeness of our family. We could not stay away very long before wanting to get back home to see them.

It was then we decided to sell our beautiful villa. At that time, we thought it was better to have lived and enjoyed the experience than not to have done it at all.

Little did I know there would be another milestone to overcome, a bolt from the blue!

Part II – 2007

I came across those words written by myself in Portugal whilst on holiday in 2007. It was an immensely happy moment sitting on the beach with my husband, simply relaxing in the midday sun, with the cool wind gently blowing by, when we looked at each other and smiled; enough to make it the most perfect moment.

That was when I put my feelings into these words.

***

Togetherness

Smiles on our faces, hearts aglow
Peace on our minds, let everyone know.
The dreams we share, days spent together
Enjoying each other, whatever the weather.

Love's sweet memories we held for a while
Paradise on Earth, this was the style!
True colours of life we lived, you and I
How great was our love, how blue was the sky.

Good times at the villa!
Living a life of happiness, carefree.
No worries for me,
Is this Heaven for me,
Is this Heaven on Earth?
Am I not lucky?

July 13th 2007

***

How was I to know what the future would hold in the coming year?

It was the same year we were selling our property in Portugal when things changed. We were having to make trips to and from England to finalise the sale of our beautiful holiday haven.

Recently, I had read an article in a women's magazine about breast cancer. It emphasised the importance of noticing any signs of lumps and if so to have them checked by the doctor.

I had noticed a lump, so before going back to Portugal, I visited my doctor who said not to worry after checking me. She presumed it was a cyst, and told me to carry on with our trip, but when we returned, she would send me for a mammogram to be sure it was not anything more serious.

The day of the mammogram came. It was only a routine check, so I was not that worried; just a little apprehensive as it was the first time I'd had a test like this. I went along with all that was needed of me, and still managed to smile, even holding a short conversation with the nurse on duty. She was very polite and helpful, so that made me relax.

Everything was going well, or so I thought.

As she checked the image on the screen, she said,

"I won't be long, dear," and left the room.

I grew worried. The time I was left on my own seemed ages.

Coming back in the room, she said, "We have to do a biopsy, but don't worry. Most probably it is nothing to be concerned about."

So I went through the biopsy with an open mind. This procedure took more time than I expected, but I thought, "Never mind." I carried on with my plan to get home on the bus. I left on my own, as that was how I had come.

I was a bit shaken after the ordeal, but as soon as I got home, I told my husband what had happened.

After a short rest, we carried on with the day. I could not help going over in my mind what had happened earlier, but decided to distract myself with things to do, preparing for my granddaughter's wedding, which was soon to come.

It was within a week that I received a letter from the hospital. An appointment had been arranged for me to see a consultant at Clinic 5.

Reading this letter, I grew worried enough to tell my daughter about the lump, at which she promptly said she would go with me as moral support, alongside my husband. Days simply raced by, as I kept my mind busy, with the arrangements for the forthcoming wedding.

All too soon it was time for the appointment.

Sitting in the waiting room, my husband and daughter either side of me, I felt very nervous. So many things were going through my mind.

What were they going to tell me? Was it something serious or not? Was I worrying needlessly?

My hands became clammy, and I squeezed hold of my handkerchief for comfort.

At the time, I daren't let my husband or my daughter know my true feelings. After all, there was a chance I might not have anything to worry about.

While we were waiting anxiously, I sat watching other people in the room. They were mostly sitting in couples. I couldn't help noticing the quiet atmosphere and solemn faces on most of them. Looking around made me even more worried.

Turn by turn, they were called. After a long while, we would see them coming out with serious faces, talking low, walking hand in hand, as they left accompanied by a nurse. I was so pleased to see two couples come out smiling. My heart lifted with joy, thinking it was not all doom and gloom.

My turn finally came. At my name being called, my heart pounded, and it made me jump. My husband firmly took hold of my hand and gave me a reassuring look. Quickly, I pulled myself together. He was ready to go in, but I said that our daughter coming with me would be okay, as she had come especially to be there for me. Inside, I was trying not to let my husband worry without reason.

The next few hours were so traumatic. I don't know how I pulled myself through. The doctor told us the tests had come back positive. I had cancer in the second stage.

He stated that there would be an operation to remove the tumour, followed by radiotherapy which would be given over short periods of time and would last for five weeks. I felt very faint and sick, thinking my heart must have stopped with the shock of the news.

My daughter took hold of my hand and said in a firm but kind way, "Mum, hold on, you will be okay, we are with you all the way."

Bless her, as she must have suffered a similar shock at the outcome, but for my sake held in her feelings.

I was given a drink of water which I found hard to swallow, but nevertheless, it did pull me together a little; just enough to hear what the rest of the treatment entailed and how it would be administered.

I was in a daze. My whole being was knocked into a pulp. By that time, my husband had been called, and between him, the doctor and my daughter, we went through the vital stages of my treatment in detail.

The doctor was very sympathetic and understanding. He did not rush at any point and slowly went through again how we could get over this cancer and beat it.

"We will try our very best," was his way of giving us something to hold on to.

As we made our way out of the hospital, my legs felt like jelly. So much went through my head at that moment. Was this really happening? What would I do? How would I cope? Would I get better? How would my family take it? God! Why did it have to happen?

My mind was racing inside with these unanswered questions, so much so, I went quiet and thoughtful. I did not want to speak or hear anyone. It was as if I was in a nightmare.

The journey home seemed like a million miles. This was the first milestone I had to overcome. One of many in the coming months.

Around me, I could feel my hands being held and words of comfort, but I chose to block out the words and actions of the people who cared. I needed to be alone, but that was not to be yet.

Finally, we arrived home. I dumped myself onto a settee and tried to stop myself from shaking. I was given a warm blanket over my legs.

Our children were called over to come and see me. They didn't know anything then, but after a while, they were told about my ill health. Bless my daughter, she kept our spirits up. My husband was quiet, suffering the same sort of shock as me, I suppose, knowing we had to face it yet another time round.

The family were so utterly shocked, silence reigned. It was as if someone had pulled the plug out of the volume in the room.

It dawned on them that this was a very serious situation we were being put through and how we coped would be crucial to us as a closely knit family.

Suddenly, the lord of the manor, my faithful husband spoke out loud and clear in an orderly way, "We must be strong for your mum."

These were powerful words that gave strength to the weakness the family was experiencing. The children pulled themselves together again and one by one, came to hug and kiss my troubles away, giving me words of comfort and encouragement.

Amongst these moments, my motherly instincts overcame the doubt, the fear and the fragility I was going through.

I smiled a weak smile and said that I would be okay. "Please don't worry about me. I will keep positive for the sake of us as a family."

I added that there would be a wedding in a few weeks, and we would carry on regardless. We would work around appointments, operations and healing. I would not let them down.

I don't know how I got to say these words, but my children gave me a special look as if to say they were proud of my courage.

The following day was full of apprehension. I

could not get over the negative thoughts preying on my mind. Questions were eating away at me, unable to be answered yet. My major worry, I was facing my worst enemy again - cancer. I already felt as if I was spiritually crushed. Would I be able to get up and fight? Did I have the strength needed for such a major catastrophe ruling my life again? I felt drained.

My worst fear, however selfish, was that I could not face having a mastectomy. It would destroy me. My womanhood would be taken away from me. My feminine looks would not be real. I would look abnormal. I would not feel whole. How would I face people? How would they feel toward me? Would I be shunned? Could I live with being pitied? All this was going on in my head - panic and mayhem.

In the day, there were times of happiness when my fears were lost in the company of those who loved and needed me. Talk of the forthcoming wedding distracted me, which was a blessing.

The nights, however, were long and lonely. Even with my husband by my side, I was alone with my thoughts. Before going to sleep, he would talk positively about what we could achieve as a couple when I got well; plans that were a part of our hopes and dreams, the desire to live them together. Eventually, sleep would take him over and he would rest. It was in the middle of the night when my senses would suddenly wake, going over everything again. I felt upset and angry. How unfair was it to be going through all of this again? Why had life dealt me another massive blow?

Then at times through my unshed tears, which were held back during the day, I would release my anguish, my distraught emotions. I could write truly and openly on blank paper, filling it in with my private fears and feelings that had become the bane of my life. These writings are still with me.

The fateful day arrived. I went to the hospital with my husband and daughter. I remember looking at them both. How strong they seemed. How strong I felt.

After admitting me, they were asked to leave. They were assured I was in good hands.

Having said goodbye, I suddenly felt very lonely, fragile and helpless. This was not for long, as nurses came to my rescue. They gave me understanding sympathetic smiles and whisked me away to occupy me with other procedures that were to be done, i.e. blood samples, temperature, medication, notes to be taken. I would class them as angels.

Next, I was taken to a ward where the bed had been made in preparation for the operation the following day. As I settled heavy-heartedly, I noticed the other beds were occupied, seven in all. I was surprised to see a few patients smiling, acknowledging me. I did manage a weak smile in reply to them. All of a sudden, conversation took over, albeit at a little softer volume than usual. Curtains were drawn around two beds. Clearly there was need for quiet in the ward.

I felt more at ease. These ladies were in a similar situation to myself. I digested the information slowly but surely. Each woman had cancer; separate stages and levels of this horrible disease. A couple had had mastectomy operations. The others were at the stage of recovering after lumpectomy surgery. They were all friendly, lovely women.

The ladies either side of my bed were at the same stage as me. They too would have their operations the next day, so the following few hours passed with short introductions and stories of how they got to this part of their treatment.

Here I was in a different world, a place that consisted of people with whom I could relate. People I could open up to, in similar situations to myself, with things in common, living, coping in our own way. It made me feel a little better in the knowledge that I was not the only one, selfish but true.

Seeing these poor women reminded me of my special friend Shirley who was also fighting this disease. I learned later that she had not won her battle. I was very sad to hear this news. I will always miss her.

This poem I wrote for her.

***

To My Special Friend

"There is a land where skies are blue,
There is a land where dreams come true,
There is a land I know, do you?
Let us call it fairyland."

We used to sing this song in school,
sitting together as often as we could.
Young in age and happiness
in our hearts for each other; close.

The land of the fairies is a make-believe land,
It's made of dreams,
Nothing is real or so it seems,
It was for us then,
A perfect wonderland.

Oh, how it was then,
Alas, it is not now,
The tables turned
The cards have shown
What life is all about.

It began that fateful time of year,
Summer sun, time for fun,
Then, the winds changed,
Brought a dark cloud over us
Robbed us of the joy we had gained.

We were told we had cancer
Within days of each other.

Looking back, my friend
I had symptoms earlier than you,
How was I to know what you were also going
through?

It came to dawn on us to carry on and be brave,
To fight the fight as one
To come through unscathed.

I know we had a massive shock
the time we were told,
We were not young and carefree then,
The day we both grew old.

We opened our hearts to each other,
Said our prayers,
We will take this journey side by side
Our pain and worry shared.

***

The next day arrived. I was feeling nervous and a little queasy before being taken to the operating theatre. On the way, I repeated to myself, "Dear God," praying for my God to help me through, for the strength to mend after this ordeal. As I went under the anaesthetic, I could forget everything. I was in the hands of our maker.

When I came to, my husband was looking down on me, his face close to mine, whispering words of love and comfort. I remember being in so much pain. The doctor did say they had put me on morphine. I would feel a little better in a short while.

Looking at myself later, I saw a drip in my arm and some tubes for drainage from the operation site. Not a pretty sight. I thought, "At least that is over." Now I needed courage to heal my internal wounds, as well as the external ones others could see. I cried tears of relief, too weak to wipe them. Silently, they fell onto my pillow. Very tired, aided by the anaesthetic, I went into a deep sleep. Visitors were not allowed until that evening to help me rest through it.

Evening visiting time passed with my husband by my side. As I was still feeling too sickly to talk too much, we gathered energy from each other's quiet presence. Silent thoughts as one meant more than words could say. Such is the power of unconditional love. We will fight this together. I remember my husband's words, and the people in a similar situation, which made my stay in hospital bearable. We talked about ourselves, heard everyone's different experiences and home situations. We exchanged addresses, phone numbers and emails. It was surprising how we all wanted to keep in touch. It was how we were, getting on with our treatment. We were in the same club. Each person was there to get better.

The curtains were drawn that day, revealing a young lady who had had two mastectomies. She was quite poorly and very emotionally upset. Understandably so, as she was a deputy head teacher in a very popular private school. It took her a while to get to talk to us. Encouraging nods of greeting from the ladies in our ward gave her the will to at least return our call of compassion. We all understood her frailties. We were all in the same position not so long ago.

I counted myself lucky not to be in her shoes. I praised her inner strength. She had endured the test of massive disfiguring surgery. She was such an amazing woman. I felt guilty about my abhorrence of losing my womanly appearance. How must she feel? I know everyone has a limit or barrier they create for themselves. This was mine. I wanted to hold on to my natural shape, my identity as a mother of five. I am glad to say she picked up, slowly recovering her stamina to carry on with her life. She had no children, but did have a loving, caring husband who was mostly by her side. I still admire her.

I suddenly reflected on the first time I suffered with cancer. It took away my youthfulness, made me old before my time, and had so many side effects. Yet slowly, I picked up the pieces and recovered. Now this was the second time around. I didn't know if I was out of the woods yet.

When I told my new friends about cancer the first time round and the traumatic episodes in my life, they were shocked. How could I have developed the dreaded C twice in different areas after such a long gap?

I learned, by expressing our personal weaknesses, we can all find compassion and understanding from others.

The next few days brought lots of different

obstacles to be overcome. There were tablets, injections, changing of bandages, checking the drains, something going on all the while. Time passed us by in the knowledge we were all in the same boat. With prayers and wishes, we hoped to survive.

It was the day of returning home from hospital. Having spent the short stay in different surroundings, I hoped to be more positive about my health. I would hold myself strong for the oncoming wedding.

My homecoming was very personal. Much appreciated by me, the rooms were full of beautiful flowers and small sentimental gifts given to me by my grandchildren to help me feel better.

They came in small groups not to overpower me, letting me get back to normality. I felt better amongst my precious family. I vowed I would be there for them and they were there for me, my lifeline.

The day before the wedding was hectic. I was not well enough to stay long at our son's house. Even though I went with my husband, I sat on a separate settee, not to be disturbed or hurt in any way. I still felt weak. The stitches were still in and the wound had not healed yet. I was grateful for the tender loving care I received to help me through the day.

After an uncomfortable night, I prayed for enough strength the next day to see our granddaughter's wedding happily as I had always imagined. I awoke with a positive mind to attend the beautiful occasion, and make memories to treasure in my heart.

There were so many dreams to fulfil yet, made before this dramatic life-affecting thunderstorm poured down on me from the heavens above. I would try to weather this storm for my family's sake, to make good from bad.

The wedding day passed without problems. As planned, everyone who came made the day special. I could see happiness and feel the warmth and closeness of our children, satisfied in knowing the whole family was there to take part in the wedding photographs. I was so happy, I shed tears of mixed emotions. I was very fortunate to be there.

My daughter kept by my side, just in case I was in need of anything. There was so much going on, and in the evening, we sent our granddaughter and husband off to start their holiday booked for Paris, leaving us all happily tired and relieved.

Back home, I could rest more easily. I welcomed my bed. Being able to relax and let myself go, the wedding had taken a lot out of me.

Now I could focus on myself.

I had to concentrate on how I was progressing.

Just two days later, I was called back for another biopsy, this time of the glands. As I had stage two cancer, there was a chance it could spread to the rest of my body via the lymph nodes. The biopsy would ascertain if this was the case. Then we were told the surgeon would remove the main glands to check for cancer.

This time round, the days felt like I was on a horror ride that I could not get off.

The biopsy found that cancer had spread to the glands. The surgeon took the necessary steps to remove all the remaining glands that side of my armpit, a procedure called auxiliary clearance. All I can remember, I was in terrible pain when I came to, so I was given morphine to help me cope.

My husband was so shocked, he raised his voice to the surgeon when he informed us that he had removed all the glands in my armpit. He said he had to use his judgment as cancer had spread and he had no other option but to remove the affected glands which were like a bunch of grapes. Better to be safe than sorry. All I could do was listen, knowing I had to heal again and recover from surgery in the armpit; so many stitches and drains.

When would this nightmare end? How much more could I take?

It was like a replay of the first operation, except there was no wedding now.

The quiet times, I spent mostly in my bedroom, reflecting on the past few weeks. My wounds were fresh and sore. I felt tired and low, with no energy to get up and see to the house. Family would visit again, bringing flowers, gifts and words of encouragement. On the outside, I would smile and be polite to those who loved me and wanted me to get better. I was grateful for their support, but I felt weak and shattered. Then there was the thought of the radiotherapy to go through and the eighty mile journey every day to hospital for nearly six weeks. A massive hurdle, second time round. I felt sick just thinking of it again.

The first time, I attended radiotherapy in hospital transport as no-one was well enough in our family to drive that far every day. Tragic circumstances had taken over our lives. The power and strength had been sucked out of us like water from a well, leaving us dry and useless. I made journeys with other people. Strangers in similar situations who became travelling companions, and later close friends.

It was a struggle to travel that same road every day. Now our journey was just the two of us, my husband sitting by my side in our car. We didn't talk constantly, so at times, silence ruled. I had so much time to think. Old wounds flared up, worn down by the knocks, still anxious, fragile, scared to face all this again.

I knew how vitally important it was having radiotherapy. It was killing the evil cancer before it killed me. I felt angry, my insides burning. I was being invaded again. I felt like screaming to the world, "It is not fair. I hate what I have become. I feel I am a tool; used, abused and left to rot and rust."

Normally, I don't have vicious, horrid, cruel thoughts about anything or anyone, but my heart blasphemes heavily when I think how many millions of people this demon has killed.

Was I to become one more on that list?

Please let this murder stop.

They say time heals. I took it in my stride. Battered defeated, exhausted, I let the days pass.

The night went by with a prayer in my heart to be strong and face what else was in store for both of us. We held each other silently and found solace in our company. Sleep inevitably came to my tired, stressed soulmate. He drifted off, breathing gently and rhythmically. As I listened to him, my sleep flew out of the window.

I lay awake, unable to rest my dry, aching eyes. Doubts and negative thoughts came to my mind to haunt me again.

Another long night over.

Another day dawned.

No matter how hard I tried to forget, questions pounded in my mind. I stayed in bed, feeling low again. However, throughout the day, my family came to visit which made me feel a little better. Inside, I knew they needed me, and they wished I was as well as before the onset of this life-threatening illness.

I was their queen. I led them on through their own trials and tribulations of life with my love, wisdom and advice. I was always there for them, as now wholeheartedly, they were for me.

That day, in the quiet of my bedroom, I put pen to paper. I wrote these words. Writing for me released my inner thoughts. I kept these poems aside, thinking should I not make it, survive, I would leave a legacy for my family to read how and what I went through.

***

Written after my operation.

I do not know yet what I have to face,
All I know is that I'm living
in the human race.

I feel so worried,
I do feel sad,
Because it hurts, and I am me,
Is that so bad?

Long is the wait,
And longer still
Is hearing if I still am ill.

The road is rough and long,
It's a hard upward climb.
But the goal at the top,
If I win, will be mine.

So strive I will,
And strive I do,
Try my best to be strong
To get me through.

God give me strength
To take it all in,
To get up and fight

To survive and win.

I look around and what do I see
My wonderful family looking at me.
I look back at them and bravely smile,
For them I will try to walk that extra mile.

At this time, silent thoughts arise
We are thinking alike,
Me of them and they of me,
Our love is pure, shared,
Bonded by care and sincerity.

Should the dark day come
To hear the worst of all this,
My heart will be strong for us,
To conquer, come out of the abyss
To deserve to hang on to
The endless love I have for them,
As what they give to me
Is worth ten out of ten.

They give to me their constant thoughts,
Care, love and time,
I know I am always in their hearts,
And forever they live in mine.

With all our faith, hope and prayer,
We will look toward better times.

***

During the next few months, I had regular check-ups.

One day as I was taking a shower, I felt a lump in the same region as before, but I mentally blocked it out and shut the door on it.

"Probably nothing to worry about," I consoled my inner self. I quickly put it out of my mind and carried on as if nothing was wrong. It was not to be. Life is not that easy. What is fated will happen.

As if God ordered it, the next clinic appointment came within a week. Check-up over, the consultant pointed out he had felt another lump in the same side as before.

What a shock! My worst fears were facing me. He went on to say that he would do a biopsy. This time, there would be no alternative but to perform a mastectomy. My heart could not breathe. What was I hearing? My husband held my hand tightly; again, a massive hurdle.

We went through the details of the operation. I had to go into hospital the coming Thursday. It was the earliest my surgeon could operate. Just two days. Time was of the essence again.

We left hospital quietly in a reflective mood, so much still going on in our life. When would it stop?

Outside, the day seemed to have grown darker. Looking up to the heavens, I saw clouds forming into all sorts of shapes. Demons; huge, great, ugly creatures were glaring down at me.

Was it my imagination? No, I could hear them.

They were laughing and saying, "We are going to eat you up slowly!"

I shrank away from these images. My heart cried, "Go away! Let me be! Get out of my life!" I was dealing with so many mixed emotions. I looked towards my husband. The love of my life was there beside me. I came back to reality. Good to come back, knowing at least I had a shoulder to lean on.

Once the family were informed of the situation, we tried not to focus on it, picking other conversations to avoid the distressing news. Even so, that night, my heart was crying, "What have I done to deserve this?" Silently, tears fell down my face, wetting my pillow. How much more could I take?

As if my husband had heard me, he said, "You have to pull yourself together, be strong, keep fighting. It's the only way. Look, I am here with you all the way, love. We have a lot to see, to do. You are part of me. I need you in my life."

The comforting hug was what I needed, with the words I will never forget.

Looking at him through the dimmed light of the bedroom, I thought how fortunate I was. He had so much faith in me. He would not, could not imagine us not being together. Our many years of living as husband and wife had been put to the test time and time again, pulled down into deepest unbreathable depths, but fortunately we had still come up for precious life-saving air.

_____ *** _____

Our marriage holds strong, through testing years,
We build our house with love, wipe away our tears,
Fill our house with laughter, hope for happier days,
Looking at our family, we are blessed in many ways.
In my life, he is my strength,
my soulmate I look up to,
Him by my side, we can still start life anew.
He will not let me go, I am his treasure,
Hand in hand, we will live together, forever.
He is my saviour, a pillar of strength,
my one and only,
To this day I thank him for his loyalty,
love, devotion to me.

_____ *** _____

———— *** ————

Results after my operation.

CLEAR

Hip Hip Hooray!
Hip Hip Hooray! Again.

I've won the race,
Become whole again.

Come out of the rain into sunshine,
Bright days, golden days,
Better days!

I will pick myself up, mend my ways
My body, my spirit, my mind will be strong,
I know now where I belong.
I will find true happiness once more,
God has opened the door,
Shown the way to again laugh and play
I humbly say, "Thank you Dear God
for another wonderful day."

Your priceless, precious gift of health
To me is worth much, much more than all our wealth.

I will not ponder on the year gone by,
It was a year of sorrow,
Mostly wondering, how and why?
Uncertain days, lonesome days,
In a maze, nothing clear, in a haze.

My battery dead,
On eggshells did I tread.

Now,
I can leave all that behind,
A new lease of life I have found,
That of a much better kind.

Fortunate and thankful, ready to accept,
Lucky am I to be able to forget.

I will try to heal the scars, mental and physical ones also.

I feel blessed and humble.

It is amazing how much one can suffer and still find some happiness in the end. I was in a sea of deep, dark waters, drowning. Somewhere there was a vessel to rescue and carry me to safe shores, a destination where my life began again and where living is now pleasurable.

Living a "normal" life again with the people I love makes all the difference in the world to me. I have gained self-esteem, enough to value and enjoy each day and live it to the full. I do not take things for granted now. Instead, I push myself to set small tasks; knitting, sewing, tidying the bedroom, even cooking, and work towards finishing them, even if it takes more time than before. Doing this gives me a sense of pride and satisfaction. My family has noticed the change in me and encourage me to keep me focused.

I can again enjoy nature and all its beauty; early morning sunrise, warm sunny days, the pitter-patter of raindrops on the window pane, feeling the cool night air. Many things I enjoyed before, such as seeing a rainbow full of vibrant colours, glowing, shining, an awesome scene, such beauty! The few minutes looking at a rainbow gives me so much pleasure.

"One day I will catch my rainbow," I used to whisper to myself. My rainbow is my "gold," an ultimate goal to achieve. When I am fulfilled with happiness, peace and contentment, I will then have reached it.

Now I am in a much better part of the world, that of my yesteryear. My lonely days are gone. I am free and happy! In my heart's mind, I can reach and touch my rainbow. How fortunate I am again. Thank you, dear God.

This is not where I want it to end. I am not selfish. I must not forget the journey I made, or the unfortunate people who did not make it through.

I cannot stop thinking of those who have lost hope, or who have not got anyone, or a reason to believe that cancer does not always win.

I would like to encourage the many who are living in the dark stages of their lives and cannot see a brighter future. I will try to be a role model for them. For them my heart goes out, not in pity, but understanding, care and wishes for their full recovery.

I hope reading about my experiences of being

diagnosed, living with cancer and surviving will be helpful to the people who have had or are going through the stages similar to mine.

To write about my fight with cancer was a very difficult thing to do. I put myself in the shoes of people whom I wished to help, and relived the sad memories buried deep inside me that I would have liked to forget. To portray them honestly and openly was like opening a sore, painful wound, yet it was a way of showing how one can hit rock bottom and still bounce back. It takes great strength, but it can be done. I had the good luck and good fortune to survive.

It would give my survival a meaning, knowing that I have been of help to them in some way.

With this urge to achieve something positive from the ups and downs in my past, I decided to put pen to paper and make a strong link in the chain of a healthy life for others to hold on to. The more links, the stronger the chain.

I have somehow found the courage and inspiration to share my grief and sorrow, remembering I was on that side of that road not so long ago.

I thank all those who stood by me in my hour of need; family and friends to whom I will be eternally grateful, and very importantly to the consultants, doctors and nurses, as without them, my recovery would not have been possible.

I have learned so much on this journey.

***

"Life is only one time round.
Live it to the full."

***

***

Reflections

Twilight Trees.

In the park looking around,
I see so much life to be found.
The evening brings the mists again.
The sky is grey, some trees are bare.
Some lucky few have still their youth,
The beauty to adorn and share,
Autumn leaves, all shades of green,
Golden browns, yellows, vivid reds,
What a colourful scene!
The leaves wear coats of dewdrops that
Dance, swaying gently in the breeze,
Then fall like silvery rain onto,
Flowerbeds and younger trees.
No matter what the shape or size,
This is true beauty to my eyes.
Trees are alive, mystical, have majesty,
Joyful! How blessed I am, this scene to see,
Standing alone am I, yet not lonely,
I feel an air of peace and tranquillity.
But, all too soon, twilight has come,
The park is silhouetted and darkness has just
begun.
Two shades of life have turned to one.
The ending of an evening sunset and,
Beginning of a new morn, the rising sun.

______ *** ______

Now and Tomorrow…22nd May, 2013

Every day is a present, like each new dawn,
Who knows what tomorrow may bring?
It truly is a mystery as,
Tomorrow has yet to be born.
Life is not a written page we must follow,
We are writing it each second of our time,
It can only be read by tomorrow,
Live life to the full, achieve your aims,
It can then read as a beautiful page,
Beautiful, satisfying lines.

______ *** ______

ND - #0269 - 080726 - C0 - 216/138/6 - PB - 9781784560584 - Matt Lamination